Born Deaf, Now Bionic

Can't Hear You, I'm Graduating

Amazing Views From Up the Hill

C M Plush

The moral rights of the author have been asserted
All rights reserved. Except as permitted under the Australian Copyright Act 1968 (for example, a fair dealing for the purposes of study, research, criticism or review), no part of this book may be reproduced, stored in a retrieval system, communicated or transmitted in any form or by any means without prior written permission. All inquiries should be made to the author.
contact: info@immortalise.com.au

© Catherine Plush 2025
Author/s: Catherine Plush
Series Title: Born Deaf, Now Bionic
Title: Can't Hear You, I'm Graduating:
   Amazing Views From Up the Hill.

ISBN: paperback   978-1-7638310-9-4
ISBN: ebook   978-1-7638310-8-7

First published in November 2025
by Immortalise, Hackham SA
Typesetting, editing and cover: Ben Morton

This is me, Catherine Plush!

Contents

What is "The Up The Hill Project"? 1
About Me 3
Why I Enrolled With Up the Hill Project ... 7
Dramas 11
What is Cerebral Palsy? 15
What are Cochlear Implants? 18
It Starts: Semester One 2023 20
Semester Two 25
2024 Semester Three 26
Semester Four 28
AGOSCI inc Conference 2025 Adelaide ... 30
25 Years of Up The Hill! 33
Semester Five 35
Semester Six 37
Foundations Course 39
What's Next? 40

What is "The Up The Hill Project"?

The Up The Hill Project is a brilliant initiative of Flinders University. It aims to support the participation of adults with a wide range of disabilities in both the social and educational life of the university. Participants receive extra help from a peer mentor to guide them through each of six topics. These topics are studied one per semester over three years.

As a part of The Up the Hill Project, the participants get to pick which six topics they study. The subjects could be anything from right across the University; from the top of Bedford Campus all the way down the hill to Sturt Campus and the huge oval on Main South Road!

I picked subjects that I knew I could be passionate about and am proud that they weren't all first year subjects. Although I was required to attend lectures and tutorials, I didn't have to do all the readings, assignments and quizzes. But I am proud to say that I did them

Can't Hear you, I'm Graduating

all anyway, because I am very brave, courageous, determined and have strong willpower.

It is exciting to think that I am the first person in the program with cerebral palsy and deafness, as well as the communication barrier caused by dysarthria. Because of The Up the Hill Project, I have grown so much as a person, my confidence has increased, and I am able to do things I never thought would be possible.

About Me

My name is Catherine. I joined the Up The Hill Project in 2023, and my motto in life is to have a laugh every day!

I am a wife, a mum and Grammy Cathy.

I was born prematurely in December 1956. Unfortunately my early birth came with some complications. I was born with severe hearing loss, cerebral palsy and dysarthria, which is a severe speech impediment due to weak muscles in my jaw and mouth.

When I was young, I attended two different special education school environments, neither of which were very academic. In fact, Ashford House School for Cerebral Palsied Children, was a day program as much for respite and general therapies as it was for academic progress. At the time there was a pool, physio and speech therapy, space to rest and space for fun! Always lots of fun!

Can't Hear you, I'm Graduating

I felt that all this held me back with my learning, but I'm not complaining as I did enjoy it. There was also the additional obstacle of my deafness. Because I didn't begin speaking until I was eleven years old. I missed out on a lot of educational opportunities, when I was younger.

I am lucky because I was very loved by my family. I could still do things on my own and was encouraged to grow into independence from a very young age at around four years.

My parents were amazing and believed I should be treated the same as the other children. They even let me go on the school bus by myself when I was just four years old! We went to church every Sunday and I felt like I was just the same as my siblings as well.

When I was in year ten, when my dad made the decision to take me out of school as he didn't feel I was able to keep up with the other girls. I didn't really know that I was going to high school to be educated, I wasn't sure why I

About Me

was there. Now, I like to think that I could have done it, if I had known back then and stayed on.

Things have changed a lot since I was a young girl. Technology, specifically assistive hearing technology, has advanced so much. I am grateful for this opportunity to learn now.

Can't Hear you, I'm Graduating

Me at Flinders University

Why I Enrolled With Up the Hill Project

I remember my brother.

Mark is dead. He died too young, with a weakened brain.

I remember Mark in his school uniform, ready for his first big day at school. He looks so happy and excited to begin. His uniform was way too big for his tiny frame, but his brain was big. His heart was just as big, and he was always quick to smile and ready with a joke.

He always had his cheeky smile and loved being with his family. I am the youngest, Mark was only one year and twelve days older. We were very close growing up and he was my special playmate.

Mark was such a gentle soul, loving and caring. He loved nature, he loved animals and he adored his family. He grew vegetables for us all to pick and eat, and took wonderful photos of us. He was my protector and was always looking out for me.

His nose was always stuck in a book or a comic. Mark was happy to spend time alone but equally happy to be with his siblings. Passionate about life, Mark would give anything a go, and he painted a few landscapes too. He was so clever and could do anything he turned his mind to.

In July 2021, Mark passed away, he died the same day as my father had ten years earlier. He had battled with early-onset dementia and Alzheimer's. I watched him deteriorate. It was extremely distressing. Where was the brother that I loved?

Why I Enrolled With Up the Hill Project

Photo of Mark with me,
Dad with JackieJack

Can't Hear you, I'm Graduating

I am haunted by the memory of him lying there, with tubes all over him. I tried to speak to him but he didn't respond. I still haven't been able to go back to the hospital he was in.

He left behind five Children and eleven Grandchildren.

His battle inspired me to keep my own brain healthy and active.

But also for me.

I want to learn. I lost eleven years of my life without the power of speech and want to make up that time now. I also want to improve my written English skills so that I can tell my story.

The story of my life is one of resilience, hard work, but also fun and family. I want this story to help break down stereotypes and misunderstandings about people with disabilities.

My hope is that my story inspires people to overcome their obstacles, to follow their dreams and to want to understand the people around them.

Dramas

My first mentor was in a wheelchair, and we would joke that I need a wheelchair too as I also had problems walking. I was suffering with plantar fasciitis, which is very, very painful!

The Flinders University Campus is huge, with so many hills, and there was always so much walking to do! I wonder if there are many more people who end up with similar issues?

I had to have an injection in my foot which was very excruciating!! Thankfully it worked and I was able to keep going.

This however was nothing compared to the serious injury I suffered in my back.

Can't Hear you, I'm Graduating

I forgot the code! They had to get security to come and unlock it for me!

Dramas

In May 2024, I was actually a "Silly-Billy-Cathy"! I can be a bit stubborn at times. I didn't listen to my hubby, and I lifted heavy weights for about five days in a row.

Then, on Monday, I couldn't get out of bed. I couldn't even lift my leg off the bed. I was screaming in pain. I had pinched a nerve in my back, which kept me in bed for six weeks. I took lots of medicine from the doctor to try and take the pain away and I pushed myself so I could go back to uni.

I tried everything the doctors asked. I went to Flinders Hospital Pain Clinic and they wanted to do an MRI scan. But this wasn't a viable option because of my cochlear implants and so they couldn't determine the damage. What could I do then?

Eventually I was able to get in and see a specialist in Norwood. They decided to operate which was able to be done in October. That was a long time of pushing through!

Can't Hear you, I'm Graduating

The operation was quite scary. Because my nerve had been squashed, they had to cut the nerve to give the vertebrae more room. My whole body felt like it was upside down, it was going crazy. It took six more months to recover as my body had to adjust to the new rhythms.

I am not going to be a "Silly-Billy-Cathy" ever again!

But I loved my learning so much that in all that time I only took one day off! Although I missed my presentation because I was booked in for the operation.

What is Cerebral Palsy?

Cerebral palsy (CP) is a condition that occurs when a baby's brain either doesn't develop properly or is damaged early in life. It can affect how the brain controls movement, posture, and muscle tone.

For me, it was due to a complication at birth as I had the wrong blood group. Because I was premature they didn't think that I would live. I was given a blood transfusion but it didn't reach my brain quickly enough.

CP affects different people in different ways and to different degrees.

People with cerebral palsy might have trouble with walking, balance, speech, or coordination. The condition can range from very mild to more severe, and it affects everyone differently.

CP is not a disease and doesn't get worse over time, but the challenges it creates can change as someone grows.

Although there is no cure, therapies, medication, and support can help improve a person's quality of life and independence.

What is Cerebral Palsy?

Me in the Kitchen

What are Cochlear Implants?

A cochlear implant is a medical device that helps people who have severe hearing loss or are deaf. Unlike regular hearing aids, which make sounds louder, cochlear implants bypass the damaged parts of the ear and send sound signals directly to the brain.

The implant has two main parts: one that is placed under the skin behind the ear during surgery, and another that sits outside the ear like a small processor. Together, they help a person detect sounds and, with training, understand speech.

Cochlear implants don't restore normal hearing, but they can make a big difference in communication, especially for children learning language or adults who've lost hearing later in life.

What are Cochlear Implants?

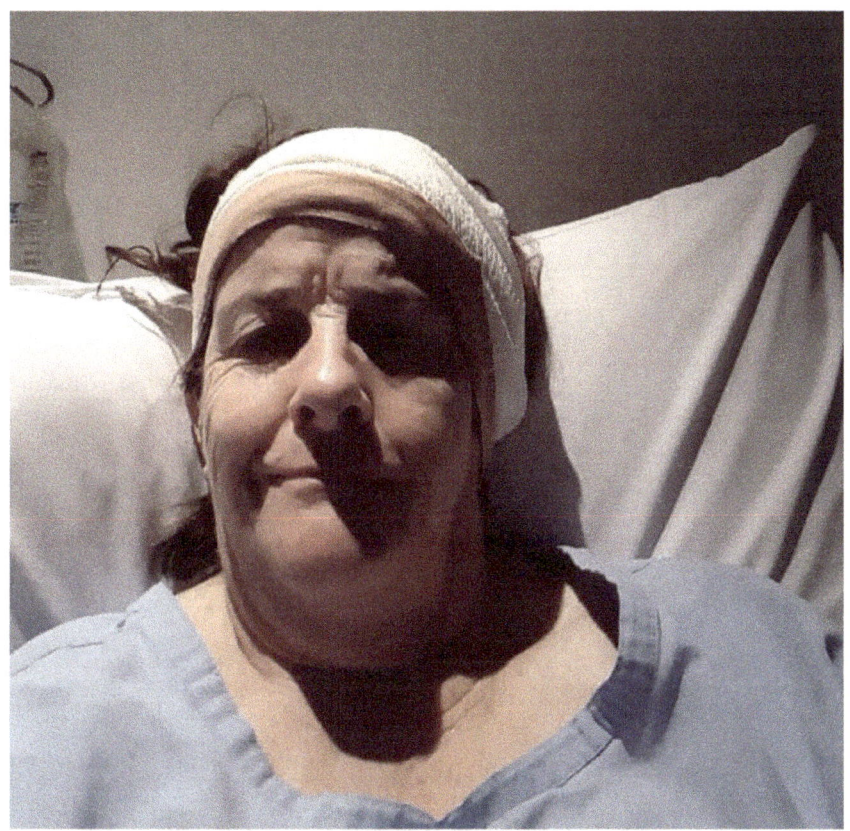

Me after the operation to get the cochlear implants

It Starts: Semester One 2023

Here I am starting university at age 66! It was completely confusing and so overwhelming. The campus is large, there are buildings everywhere and lots of big trees that made me feel small and lost in a massive university.

Trying to find my tutorial room was like a nightmare maze. It felt like it just went on and on and on. I could have fainted - which would have been funny!

The walking was quite full on. I did get used to it, and know it was good for me - very healthy! In fact, I think I got fitter from time at university. Maybe I could do a marathon now? Ha ha! Only joking!

Everywhere I went it was crowded, there were just so many people! Everyone was busy, it reminded me of crossing the road at the traffic lights of a busy intersection. I have worked in busy kitchens, but this felt much bigger and intimidating.

It Starts: Semester One 2023

I am thankful that I was able to have my mentor, Anna, to guide me through it. Her help and kindness built me up so that I could find my feet and make my own way through university life.

Can't Hear you, I'm Graduating

Semester one with Anna

It Starts: Semester One 2023

Writing in the 21st Century:

I chose this topic to help improve my written English skills, knowing that I planned to put my memoir together.

Because I left school in year 10, I felt like I wasn't educated enough to write something worthwhile. This wasn't something that had really bothered me in the past. It wasn't until my brother died that I realised how much I wanted to be able to pass on my story to my two grandsons, before it's too late! You don't know when your time will be up.

In addition, my deafness and speech impediment made me feel as though I was behind everyone else. My grandson is currently five and a half years old and he can talk better than I can. Maybe I should have asked him to do my presentations for me!

Professor Kate Douglas was lovely and incredibly experienced with her topics. She made lectures, tutorials and activities easily accessible, doing things like adding subtitles so I could learn more efficiently. I credit her with my success in that first semester. There had been a part of me that was surprised I made it through.

My favourite part of the course was when I got to write a story. I chose to write a short biography about myself as a starting point for my memoirs! What a great way to show to myself that I CAN do this!

Semester Two

I completed the topic 'Life Writing' with Professor Kate Douglas. This topic reviewed the history and different genres of writing about someone's life - such as confessions, poetry, letters, diaries, biographies, memoirs and even photography! The list keeps going!

We learnt about lots of different themes. I found self-identity, memory and trauma, and the moral and legal issues surrounding self-representation in writing the most interesting to learn about.

This topic really fuelled my inspiration to write my memoir!

Throughout this semester I was lucky enough to have two mentors. They were both called Emily! This got a bit confusing for me so I called them Emily #1 and Emily #2. Emily #2 ended up being my main mentor through this time and she was fabulous!

2024 Semester Three

This year it was time to start my journey into disability studies. These classes are held at the Sturt campus, which was a very different experience to last year. I was so impressed with all the lecturers. They were so passionate about supporting and uplifting the disability community!

I started with the topic 'Perspectives on Disability' with Demi and Jamie as my lecturers. I found this topic so interesting because it focused on the lived experience of disability as well as the different attitudes towards diversity and disability and the effects these can have.

Something I found particularly interesting was my own self-realisation! Despite having lived with a disability my whole life, there were still times where I displayed 'ableism' or 'othering' - towards myself or others - without even realising!

2024 Semester Three

I found this topic so much more accessible and my two lecturers were very aware and understanding towards people with disabilities. I really appreciated how these lecturers were flexible around their issues as well as mine.

Attending these tutorials was also very different. Many of the students had their own lived experiences or had family members that have disabilities too. I felt that they were much more accepting to have me in their class.

I also got to experience a new kind of mentor! Yi was from Malaysia, she was studying Speech Pathology. She loved to have fun and was very active in the social scene. She could speak four different languages. Impressive!

Semester Four

Three down and three to go, I am officially half way there!

I continued my disability studies with the subject 'Communication Rights and Access.' I am particularly passionate to learn more about Augmentative and Alternative Communication (AAC). It makes me excited to think that one day I may be able to access the best assistive technology to assist me to communicate more effectively!

This topic was very special to me. I am so grateful that my professor was so caring and supportive, helping to make it as easy as possible for me to learn more. This included adding subtitles and being available to explain and simplify anything that I was confused with. Plus things were put into 'Easy Read Format' or even had adjusted instructions for me!

I was really proud to be a part of this subject which was a 3rd year topic! And my lecturer was also really proud of me. Dr Eleanor Watson even helped me to apply and ultimately receive a scholarship to a conference held in town in 2025. She was the best!

AGOSCI inc Conference 2025 Adelaide

For three hot days in March, I went to the Festival Theatre to attend this amazing conference.

There were so many stalls and people there who came from all over Australia to attend. I was able to see demonstrations of different products.

Dr Watson, my lecturer, was one of the speakers at the event! I was able to hear her speak about AAC research which was so exciting.

There were a lot of workshops and presentations across the three days. It was wonderful to be a part of how accessible and inclusive they all were. And there was always plenty of exceptional food available to keep us fuelled up!

On Friday night the conference hosted a special social dinner. It was completely booked out but I wouldn't let that stop me! My patience paid off when some people cancelled and I was able to get a last minute ticket to attend. I was very fortunate!

The lights made it so colourful and the dance-floor was packed out. Some people got dressed up and had their photos taken. One of the ladies who was dancing actually went to the same school as me when we were children and I am happy to say that we've been able to become friends again.

It was such a good learning experience.

Can't Hear you, I'm Graduating

My photo from the conference

25 Years of Up The Hill!

In September 2024, Flinders University celebrated 25 years of the Up The Hill Project! I was so happy to be there for the celebrations. There were politicians who came along and a big ceremony.

I was one of only four students who were picked to do a presentation about our topics. We were standing at the back of the auditorium waiting for our turn to speak. When we were introduced everyone turned around to see us.

What did I do?

I fell over!

Thank you to everyone who jumped up to help me out. I was all OK, just embarrassed. But, I will be the one they all remember!

Can't Hear you, I'm Graduating

25 years presentation

Semester Five

For Orientation Week I caught the bus to uni. Unfortunately I got on the wrong bus that was express from Happy Valley, all the way into Adelaide!! I was late for my first day!

The topic I took was 'Interpersonal and Interprofessional Communication.' It focused on how to speak with clients when they come in. My teacher was Olwyn Riquier, I found her very supportive with everyone. She was a very good lecturer who knew her topic.

My mentor for this subject was Olivia who met with me each Monday for fourteen weeks.

The main reason I took this subject was to help with my public speaking and to give me more confidence. They gave so many tips. I printed ALL the information they gave me! We did a couple of role play exercises which I thought were fun. It was a good break from just having the lecturer talking.

Can't Hear you, I'm Graduating

Talking about how to talk to other people was confusing at times!

For our group assignment I was in charge of putting together an electronic presentation. This meant that I didn't have to talk too much in front of everyone. I was able to use the speech tool in the presentation to read out my part of the speech.

Semester 5 with Olivia

Semester Six

As I write, I am actually studying this very last semester of The Up The Hill Project. My topic... 'The Psychology of Weird and Wonderful Ideas!!'

This topic has Dr Kenneth Sim at the head of the team, but he brought in guest lecturers every week. I loved the lecture on sleep "Myth-Perceptions About Sleep"! Also "Why We Get Happier As We Get Older", really good!! In fact there were so many great topics.

This semester was the first time I was in a lecture room that was set up on such a steep angle. The view from the top of the stairs made me feel like I might fall. Thankfully, I really needed to sit in the front row each week to ensure that I could hear everything and see without other students blocking my view.

Each week we needed to do an in-class reflection and quizzes and then there was one major assignment. The reflections each week I found to be easier than doing assignments and

Can't Hear you, I'm Graduating

it felt like I could get it over and done with, without as much stress.

My mentor this semester was a really clever lady from Nepal who was studying her Masters. Subi would work weekends, plus studying and doing her placement! I can't imagine trying to do it all! I hope she gets some rest during the holidays.

Semester 6 with Subi

Foundations Course

With my last Semester, I decided to attempt a free Flinders University Foundation Course.

Crazy Cathy had only ten weeks to complete an essay from scratch to over 1000 words and also to put together a group PowerPoint presentation with four other students as well.

What's Next?

First on the list, I am looking forward to my mock graduation. I am writing this book in dedication to my youngest brother, Mark, as well as my loving Dad and Mum.

I have loved my university experience so much that I decided to continue my education with the Flinders Foundations Course! And, to make it easier for people to access, it is free!

PLUS! I will continue to keep working on my memoirs!

This time with Flinders University has given me so much confidence and the skills I need to make my dream of becoming an author come true.

I hope that this book inspires many others to follow their dreams!

What's Next?

What's Next?

This is just the first in a series of books I'm writing

Can't Hear you, I'm Graduating

www.ingramcontent.com/pod-product-compliance
Lightning Source LLC
Chambersburg PA
CBHW061212070526
44583CB00025B/3222